21st Century Skills Library

COOL SCIENCE CAREERS

ASTRONAUT

KELLY MILNER HALLS

Published in the United States of America by
Cherry Lake Publishing, Ann Arbor, Michigan
www.cherrylakepublishing.com

Content Adviser
Dr. Richard P. Hallion, Aerospace Historian

Credits
Photos: Cover and pages 1, 4, 6, 9, 12, and 28, Photo courtesy of NASA; page 10,
©ImageState/Alamy; page 15, ©NASA Images/Alamy; page 16, ©AP Photo/NASA,HO;
page 18, ©The Photolibrary Wales/Alamy; page 20, ©Michael Doolittle/Alamy; page 23,
©AP Photo/Itsuo Inouye; page 24, ©AP Photo/NASA/JPL-Caltech; page 26, ©Sharon
Dupuis/Alamy

Library of Congress Cataloging-in-Publication Data
Halls, Kelly Milner, 1957–
   Astronaut / by Kelly Milner Halls.
      p. cm.—(Cool science careers)
   Includes index.
   ISBN-13: 978-1-60279-502-0
   ISBN-10: 1-60279-502-9
   1. Astronautics—Vocational guidance—Juvenile literature. 2. Astronauts—Juvenile
literature. I. Title. II. Series.
   TL793.H3422 2010
   629.45—dc22   2008047269

Cherry Lake Publishing would like to acknowledge
the work of The Partnership for 21st Century Skills.
Please visit *www.21stcenturyskills.org* for more information.

TABLE OF CONTENTS

ASTRONAUT

CHAPTER ONE

WHAT IS AN ASTRONAUT?

Name one person who hasn't looked up at the starry night sky in wonder. It might not be easy to do. People all over the world are struck by the mystery of space.

Space is filled with mysteries waiting to be solved.

For some people, an interest in space leads them to pursue a very exciting career as an astronaut. But what do astronauts actually do? And how did the very first astronaut get his start?

LIFE & CAREER SKILLS

Space travel would not be possible without computers. Computer equipment helps run life-support systems for astronauts. It also helps astronauts in space and experts on Earth to navigate spacecraft. With all the roles that computers perform in space travel, it's very important for astronauts to be comfortable with this high-tech equipment. What are some steps someone your age could take to advance your skills with computers and technology?

Before we answer these questions, let's examine the origins of the word *astronaut*. In Latin, *astronaut* means "star sailor." The term was used by author Percy Greg in 1880 to describe a fictional spacecraft. About 100 years earlier, the word *aeronaut* referred to a person who flew hot air balloons.

Today, astronauts are people who travel to and work in outer space. The history of the modern astronaut began to take shape in 1958. That's when President Dwight D. Eisenhower created the National Aeronautics and Space Administration (NASA).

Buzz Aldrin was the second man to set foot on the moon.

The Soviet Union was a country made up of Russia and several other countries. In 1957, the Soviet Union launched an unmanned space satellite called *Sputnik*. This worried many Americans, so Eisenhower created NASA to help the United States catch up. The "space race" was born.

Cosmonauts are astronauts from Russia or the former Soviet Union. In April 1961, cosmonaut Yuri Gagarin became the first man to orbit Earth aboard *Vostok 1*. One month later, Alan Shepard made his *Freedom 7* spacecraft flight. Shepard became the first American to enter space. The historic flight lasted 15 minutes.

Who would be the first astronaut to walk on the moon? In 1962, President John F. Kennedy announced that he wanted to lead the United States across that finish line first.

The road to the moon was dotted with excitement. There were also moments of tragedy. In January 1967, astronauts Gus Grissom, Ed White, and Roger Chaffee were killed in a launchpad fire. They were performing advance testing for the first *Apollo* mission.

Two years later, Kennedy's mission was accomplished. In July 1969, Neil Armstrong and Buzz Aldrin became the first men to walk on the moon. A third crewmate, Michael Collins, maintained orbit aboard their *Apollo 11* spacecraft.

Since the 1980s, American astronauts have escaped Earth's **atmosphere** using a space shuttle rather than the one-use rockets of earlier decades. The space shuttle takes off

vertically, like a rocket. But it lands horizontally, like an air-
plane. Once in space, astronauts perform complicated experiments. Throughout the history of space travel, astronauts
have shared the same spirit of wonder and adventure. And
others stand in line to follow their lead.

LIFE & CAREER SKILLS

Astronauts must have good science skills to be
able to carry out experiments in space. They must
be able to think quickly in case of emergencies.
Can you think of some other skills that would be
important to succeed as an astronaut?

The space shuttle Challenger cruises in space. Clouds block the astronauts' view of Earth.

CHAPTER TWO
ON THE JOB

W hat does it take to become an astronaut? And what does an astronaut actually do, besides rocket into space?

Men and women have to apply to become astronauts the same way people apply for any other job. About 3,500

Biology is one of the many subjects that future astronauts can choose to study.

applicants compete every two years for only 20 trainee positions. Each applicant must meet some strict requirements to be considered.

Physical fitness is crucial to becoming a successful astronaut. Space travel and missions can be physically demanding. Officials want to make sure that astronauts are strong and healthy.

A few other physical characteristics are also required. Job candidates must have 20/20 vision with or without corrective eyewear. In other words, you can wear glasses to meet the standard. Depending on the position, astronauts must be between 58.5 and 76 inches (148.6 and 193 centimeters) tall.

Education is another factor that affects who makes it as an astronaut trainee. Each applicant must have a bachelor's degree from an accredited college or university. Degrees should be in the fields of **engineering, biological** science, physical science, or math. Applicants must also have three years of professional experience in their chosen field or advanced educational degrees.

Once accepted into the training program, future astronauts spend two full years learning the NASA basics. They also learn the essentials of survival in space. The lucky few who are chosen for space travel handle a variety of duties.

Some astronauts are commanders. They are pilots who direct the launch and re-entry of the craft itself. They are also in charge of the other members of their team. Other astronauts are scientific or engineering experts. They are assigned special tasks of their own. Take, for example, an astronaut trained as a biologist. She might study how exercise in space—without the force of gravity—impacts the human body.

An astronaut trained as an engineer might be asked to make space station repairs. Imagine the courage necessary

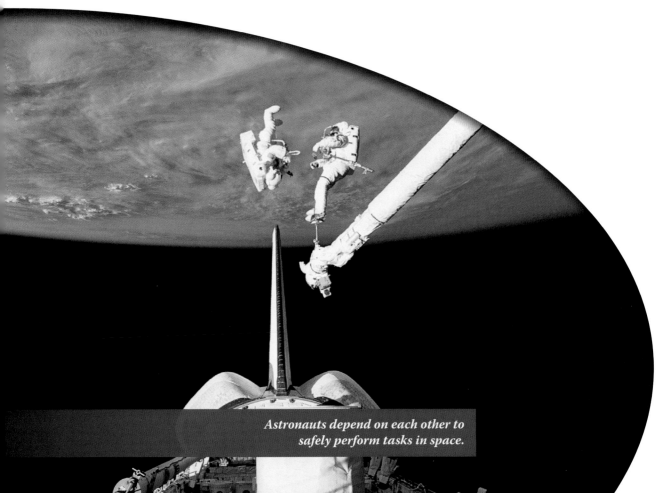

Astronauts depend on each other to safely perform tasks in space.

to float out of the shuttle hatch to perform repairs, even if a safety tether has been carefully attached. One thing that makes it less frightening is the suits astronauts wear out in space.

21ST CENTURY CONTENT

NASA selects only the best and brightest applicants to become astronauts. If you don't have excellent grades or aren't fit and healthy, you won't make the cut. Does that mean you have to give up your dreams of rocketing into space? Not if you have enough money. Thanks to space tourism, you might be able to buy your way into space.

Space Adventures is a business dedicated to giving private citizens a chance to experience space travel. In 2008, video game designer Richard Garriott paid $30 million for a first class ticket from the company. He traveled to the International Space Station aboard a Russian spacecraft. Do you think that private space travel is a good idea? Why or why not?

Human bodies are designed for life on Earth. They're made to breathe our atmosphere, which is a blend of oxygen and nitrogen. They're made to withstand the force of Earth's gravity. And they're made to function in perfect balance against the pressure the atmosphere applies to every square inch of the body.

21ST CENTURY CONTENT

The International Space Station (ISS) has been built and manned by specialists from all over the world. Experts from countries such as the United States, Russia, Italy, France, Canada, and Japan have boarded the station. In May 2008, Japan made a major contribution.

Kibo means "hope" in Japanese. It is also the name of a Japanese, **cylinder**-shaped space lab. Kibo is as big as a rock-band tour bus and as heavy as four adult elephants. The addition of this lab to the ISS will help scientists do more research in space.

One of the amazing things about the ISS is that it is truly international. The giant space station represents just one achievement that can occur when experts from around the world combine their knowledge and work together.

The spacesuits worn by the first astronauts look very different from the ones worn by today's astronauts.

When we leave the conditions of our planet, we have to re-create them in space in order to survive. An astronaut's space suit is called an Extravehicular Mobility Unit (EMU). With a price tag of $12 million, each space suit re-creates the atmosphere and pressure conditions we experience on Earth.

In the early days of space travel, the astronauts wore their space suits most of the time they were in space. These days, they are only used for missions outside the spacecraft or the International Space Station (ISS).

Space suits have some interesting features. A tiny slot near the astronaut's mouth makes it possible to slide a paper-thin fruit or cereal bar in. But most astronauts eat before they step into the suits. A special bag full of water is

Astronaut Daniel Tani has his helmet adjusted as he prepares for a space shuttle launch.

always mounted inside the suit. A tube from the bag snakes up to the astronaut's face so she can always take a sip.

How do astronauts answer nature's call when they are working in outer space? To put it bluntly, they just go! A Maximum Absorption Garment (MAG) is another name for a space diaper. It is worn under the EMU and disposed of once the space walk is over.

While astronauts are inside their pressurized work stations, they wear ordinary clothes. But when astronauts take off or return to Earth, they wear orange entry suits with long underwear underneath.

Astronauts sometimes act as delivery people. They travel into space to bring crucial supplies to their fellow astronauts at the ISS. And, of course, a few very lucky astronauts get to join the ISS team.

When they're not in space, American astronauts sometimes work as teachers. They may help train new recruits. They may also visit television stations and schools, or even ride floats in holiday parades.

Astronauts may perform many different tasks, but they share something in common. Astronauts risk their lives to do what they do. They are dedicated men and women who explore space to benefit those anchored safely back home on Earth.

CHAPTER THREE

EDUCATION AND TRAINING

If your sights are set on the stars, how can you prepare for a job in space? All astronauts agree that hard work in school is essential.

If you dream of becoming an astronaut, pay close attention in your science classes.

"You should study math and science," astronaut Sally Ride said in an interview. "It's not so important to pick one particular area of science. NASA is looking for scientists with backgrounds in all areas. But what is important is to find some area in science or engineering that is very interesting to you, and to pursue it and study it very hard."

Don't be afraid to ask questions—or to search for answers. Science and math can be fun when imagination takes hold. Be curious and determined. Learn all you can. While you're geared up for learning, be sure to study astronomy. There is so much to learn about space and the planets.

Remember those physical fitness requirements? Stay active and make fitness a part of your life. That doesn't mean you can't play video games. They can improve your hand-eye coordination, an important skill for NASA pilots and other astronauts. Just don't overdo it. Make sure that video games don't get in the way of staying active or studying.

Astronauts who command missions are also pilots. So learn as much as you can about aviation. How do airplanes work? Read lots of good books about flying. Even books about birds could help you understand the science of flight.

Are you a member of any clubs? Join an astronomy club to study planets and stars with telescopes and star charts. Or try an aviation club with other kids who want to learn about airplanes. There are also clubs for kids who like to build rockets. You might even get the chance to launch rockets on your own or as a team.

If you want to take your astronaut studies to a whole new level, Space Camp may be an option to explore. The U.S. Space & Rocket Center is located in Huntsville, Alabama. Space Camp gives kids ages 9 to 18 the chance to experience spaceflight simulations and other activities. Rates aren't

Space Camp is a great way to learn more about what it is like to be an astronaut.

cheap. Prices run between $600 and $900, not including the transportation costs from your home to the camp.

Once you're old enough, learn how to fly a small plane. If you are really excited about being a pilot, consider a career in the armed services. Some astronauts are selected from military ranks. These men and women must have science, math, or technology-related degrees.

LEARNING & INNOVATION SKILLS

A strong background in math and science is crucial for astronauts. But it is also important to be well rounded. That's why future astronauts should also work to develop strong communication skills. Astronauts—and all scientists—need to be able to express themselves clearly. Astronauts do very important research. They must communicate their findings accurately.

But strong speaking and writing skills do not just help astronauts present their research. Communicating clearly also helps astronauts work well as a team. Members of that team could be researching in space or working hard on Earth. Solid communication skills are important tools that can help astronauts complete successful missions.

The future of the manned space program depends on the astronauts of tomorrow. Cling to your goal. Don't lose your determination. The path to becoming an astronaut is a challenging one. Very few people make it to the finish line. But if you work very hard and don't give up, your dream of a mission to space could become reality.

LIFE & CAREER SKILLS

Astronauts spend a lot of time away from friends and family on Earth. A stay at the International Space station can take several months. Experts think a mission to Mars would take a person one and a half years. How does an astronaut keep from getting homesick?

There are ways to stay connected. Special tools like the Softphone and the Orbital Communications Adapter use Internet connections so astronauts can call or e-mail people back home. The connection isn't perfect, but it helps. Astronauts also have each other, and there is always work to do. What else can astronauts do to make time away from home easier?

Some astronauts begin
their careers in the military.

CHAPTER FOUR
THE NEXT LEVEL

Space shuttles have been blasting into space since the 1980s. But the Space Shuttle Program will come to an end by 2010. So what's next for astronauts in the 21st century? What's on the horizon of space exploration?

A model of a Mars science laboratory is tested at NASA's Jet Propulsion Laboratory in Pasadena, California.

For one thing, NASA plans to develop new transportation systems for sending people and equipment into space. The space shuttle will be replaced by the crew exploration vehicle (CEV). The CEV should be ready around 2012.

There are also plans to send astronauts back to the moon by 2020. Before that happens, special equipment will study the moon. Possible landing sites will be evaluated. Equipment will also search for any natural resources. Crews of four will then be sent to the moon to help build housing.

Scientists will need to develop a system for powering a **lunar** settlement. After all, nighttime in certain areas of the moon can last for several hundred hours. But experts are working hard to perfect ways of providing energy and electricity for a settlement. Someday, missions on the moon could last as long as 180 days. Imagine the type of research and study that could be done in that period of time!

But trips to the moon could be just the beginning. Living or researching on the moon can give scientists a better idea of what it is like working in a strange, unnatural environment. This will be great experience for future explorations to even farther destinations. In 2004, President George W. Bush announced the possibility of a manned mission to Mars. Preparing for that long and dangerous journey requires a careful series of unmanned missions. This includes the launch of the Mars Science Laboratory (MSL). It's a robotic lab on wheels, complete with a laser to evaporate rocks.

MSL will become the most high-tech equipment ever sent to Mars.

Experts are developing the laser devices that will split Martian rocks into tiny bits. They will then identify the minerals that might harbor tiny fossils of ancient life. Eventually, the astronauts of the future will know which rocks to search for on Mars to collect better samples. This type of research will help scientists determine if microscopic life ever existed—or

An unmanned rover took this image of the surface of Mars.

still exists—on Mars. Scientists aren't sure when humans will be able to travel to Mars. But some experts believe the earliest date for a manned mission would be around 2030.

LEARNING & INNOVATION SKILLS

Someday in the not-too-distant future, astronauts could be building a base on the surface of the moon. Sounds impossible, right? After all, there's no water to mix cement. And it would be too expensive to fly the materials up with the astronauts. So how can scientists solve that problem?

Some experts suggest making concrete out of moondust. By mixing the lunar soil with heated liquid sulfur, the dust binds together to make space concrete. The sulfur is taken from the moondust itself.

Building a lunar outpost will take some creative thinking. Using lunar soil to make concrete is just one example of how original ideas can bring an amazing concept one step closer to reality.

Whatever the future holds for space exploration, one thing is certain: more countries will join in the adventure. China,

Japan, India, and other countries are all developing their own space programs. They plan to have astronauts on the moon by the mid- to late 2020s. Astronauts are the brave pioneers of the 21st century. A career as an astronaut is very challenging but very exciting, too. Maybe one day, you'll become a part of the special group of men and women who have explored the mysteries of space.

Maybe one day you will walk in space, too!

SOME FAMOUS ASTRONAUTS

Michael P. Anderson (1959–2003) was an African American astronaut and **payload** commander from Washington State. He died in February 2003 when the space shuttle *Columbia* broke apart during re-entry.

Neil Armstrong (1930–) was the first person to set foot on the moon. He spoke the famous words, "That's one small step for man, one giant leap for mankind." He made that historic step on July 20, 1969, the fourth day of the *Apollo 11* mission.

Yuri Gagarin (1934–1968) became the first man to orbit Earth in April 1961. While in space, he whistled the song "The Motherland Hears, The Motherland Knows." Afterward, he became a national hero in his homeland, Soviet Russia.

John Glenn (1921–) had a long career in the military, as an astronaut, and as a U.S. senator. He was the first American to orbit Earth. In 1998, he became the oldest man, at 77, to fly on a space shuttle mission.

Sally Ride (1951–) answered an ad in the newspaper seeking astronaut applications. In 1983, the gifted **physicist** and California native became the first American woman in space. Two Soviet women had already blazed the trail for female astronauts: Valentina Tereshkova in 1963, and Svetlana Savitskaya in 1982. Ride is dedicated to encouraging girls to study math and the sciences.

Alan Shepard (1923–1998) was the first American man in space. His flight was an important one. Many Americans felt encouraged that the United States would be able to catch up with the Soviet Union's space program. During a later mission, Shepard became the fifth person to walk on the moon.

GLOSSARY

atmosphere (AT-muhss-feer) the layer of gases that surrounds a planet

biological (bye-oh-LOJ-i-kuhl) having to do with biology, the science of living things and life processes

cylinder (SIL-uhn-dur) a shape that has flat, circular ends and is shaped like a tube

engineering (en-juh-NEER-ing) the application of scientific, mathematical, and technological knowledge to practical human needs

lunar (LOO-nur) having to do with the moon

payload (PAY-lohd) cargo carried by spacecraft that is needed for a space mission

physicist (FIZ-uh-sist) a scientist who specializes in physics, the science of energy and matter

FOR MORE INFORMATION

BOOKS

Elish, Dan. *NASA*. New York: Marshall Cavendish Benchmark, 2007.

Flammang, James M. *Space Travel*. Ann Arbor, MI: Cherry Lake Publishing, 2009.

Thomson, Sarah L. *Astronauts and Other Space Heroes*. New York: Smithsonian/Collins, 2007.

WEB SITES

NASA—The Clickable Spacesuit
www.nasa.gov/audience/foreducators/spacesuits/home/clickable_suit.html
Learn more about what astronauts wear during space missions

National Aeronautics and Space Administration (NASA)
www.nasa.gov/
Read about the history of NASA and its exciting plans for future space exploration

Space Camp—Space Programs
www.spacecamp.com/category.php?cat=Space
Check out some cool programs for young people interested in learning more about astronaut activities

INDEX

ABOUT THE AUTHOR

Kelly Milner Halls is the author of 25 books including innovative nonfiction about dinosaurs, mummies, albino animals, horses, dogs, zoos, and cryptozoology. She lives in Spokane, Washington.